How to Sell on Etsy With Instagram

Selling on Etsy Made Ridiculously Easy Vol.4

by Charles Huff
Founder, Craft Biz Insider

Published in USA by: Craft Biz Insider

Charles Huff

ISBN-13: 978-1-970119-22-0
ISBN-10: 1-970119-22-5

Table of Contents

About the Author

Charles Huff is a former cubicle drone turned full-time Etsy seller.

He is also the owner of the world's most neurotic Jack Russell Terrier.

A Special FREE Gift for You!

If you'd like FREE instant access to my special report "Top 10 Marketing Tools Every Etsy Seller Should Use" then head over to **CraftBizInsider.com/Free**.

(What else you gonna do? Watch another "Twilight" movie?!)

Prologue: Why Instagram is So Freakin' Awesome for Us Etsy Sellers

"Do not fear failure, but rather fear not trying."

-Roy T. Bennett

I didn't want to write this book.

I wanted nothing to do with Instagram.

I thought Instagram, the social network that appointed Kim Kardashian as its patron saint, was too:

- Shallow
- Millennial

- Smartphone-driven
- Young (way younger than me)
- Image-obsessed
- Superficial
- Full of NOTHING but pictures of Nordstrom purses and body builders showing off their abs (#SixPackOfGlory)

And that might all be true. (Especially the bodybuilding pics. Man, do guys love to show off their abs.)

But then a colleague of mine – okay, it was my 19-year old niece – showed me the startling power (and marketing effectiveness) of this new, though highly-consumed social network.

She demonstrated how simple pictures, touched up with easy-to-use filters and paired with relevant hashtags, can create stunning photos of our Etsy creations that get shared (and re-shared) to hundreds, if not thousands, of potential customers in a matter of hours. (All without spending a single dollar in advertising.)

She illustrated how brain-dead simple it was to acquire a legion of Instagram followers/fanatics, and how to create regular, consistent content that engages and inspires folks to get off their duff – and buy our stuff. (Look at that! I made a rhyme.)

And…my 19-year-old niece also, without knowing, helped me realize there's a slew of young people out there – anyone under 35 is "young" to me – who despite their reputation for being digitally-obsessed and having thc attention span of a gnat…

…crave tangible, authentic and inspiring experiences with the products they buy.

I know you don't believe me.

I know you think the analog, pre-digital world is going the way of the "8-track." And there's little room for handcrafted items in a world populated by fart-noise apps and smartphone games that make you Krush Kandy.

But I'm telling you, with every nostalgic, album-loving bone in my body, the more automated and technological the world becomes…

…the more desperately people want (need) our handcrafted creations.

And Instagram is the ultimate tool for cutting through the digital clutter — yeah, I know Instagram is part of that clutter — and presenting our Etsy offerings in the most powerful and effective way possible.

And anything that helps make our marketing more powerful, quick and effective I'm all for.

So, if you're looking for the ultimate Instagram guide that will make you a social media expert — and get you a Ph.D. in digital marketing studies — then I'm afraid you have the wrong book.

There are plenty of other well-meaning — mostly boring — Instagram books out there.

But if you're looking for a quick, down-and-dirty (not too dirty, mind you) guide that will teach you the least you need to know to use Instagram to sell more of your stuff on Etsy…

…then stick around.

Can't promise you'll get as many followers as a Kardashian. But I can promise you'll have the tools and insight to navigate this strange, though profitable, social network.

And that's worth enduring a few six-pack ab selfies, ain't it?

Chapter 1: Total Newbie, Beginner's Guide to All Things Instagram

"The beginning is the most important part of the work."

-Plato

Using a new app can be confusing. Hell, using *anything* on a smartphone can be confusing.

Still not sure how to use that "voice control" on my iPhone…and it's been THREE YEARS!

Worry not: If you've never used Instagram before and you're feeling worried about diving in, don't be. We've got your back.

Or if you've used Instagram, but had no idea

what you were doing, worry not! We will go over everything.

If you're a complete Instagram expert — and just looking for ninja marketing strategies — then skip to Chapter 2.

You're busy and have other things to do.

But for the rest of ya'll, here's a straightforward, beginner's guide FAQ to the swirling vortex that is Instagram.

What the $^@%@ is an Instagram?

Instagram is a social media platform, much like Twitter or Facebook, where you connect with friends (and strangers) by sharing pictures and videos of your latest creations — or anything else you like — with followers, friends and the REST of the Instagram world.

Why the Heck is Instagram So Frickin' Popular?

Instagram has a simple, user-friendly interface

that's easy to scroll for a society with has no attention span…err, I mean…a culture that appreciates the visual nature of things.

This means Instagram is:

- **Easy-to-use.** Unlike Twitter or Facebook, Instagram allows users to see, through a beautiful photo or video, what their favorite crafters and friends are up to.
- **Super-visual.** Instagram allows you to add cool filters, and do minor edits quickly and easily, as you post your image. This enables you to add creativity to an already-awesome shot. (Filters can also hide blemishes or enhance a curious detail within your post.)
- **Free and fun.** Instagram is free, easy to navigate. With so many people all over the world using Instagram, it's the perfect way to reach potential buyers without paying a single penny.
- **Mobile.** Loading pictures is as simple as taking a snap right on your phone, choosing a filter, adding a caption and hitting "share." Your picture loads quickly, and you can tag people, add a location and simultaneously share your post on Facebook, Twitter, Tumblr and Flickr. (All before you can say..."What's Kim Kardashian's talent,

again?")

How Can It Help Me Sell Stuff?

A beautiful photo can evoke powerful emotions that a muddled Facebook post or tweet can't do.

An Instagram user might scroll through their feed when they stop on a beautifully lit teapot fresh from your kiln, highlighted by the perfect Instagram filter. Suddenly, they're in love with your stuff.

Within your profile, they click on a link to your Etsy shop and next thing you know, they're buying a couple of your pieces. That's the power of Instagram.

And, in most cases, it didn't cost you a dime.

You can follow other artists who share your same artistic vibe. When you comment on their posts, you get your brand out there and accessible to their loyal following.

You can also use super-sneaky strategies to find followers of your fellow Etsians, but more on that later.

How Does Instagram Work?

It's a good question. And I don't want to overwhelm you with info. (We're gonna cover all the in-depth strategies as we go.) But here's the LEAST you need to know about Instagram:

- **You'll (most likely) need a mobile device**. You can access Instagram using your **desktop** or **laptop**, but Instagram is designed for a mobile platform and many features are only accessible through a phone or tablet.
- **Posting is a 4-step process**. It works like this: **1)** You head to Instagram and post an attractive photo, or video, of what's going on in your world. **2)** Add handy-dandy filters to help your picture stand out. **3)** Add simple text to accompany your image that helps your photo get noticed. (These are called captions.) **4)** People who follow you, or find your post via a search, can then "like" your picture and caption and/or leave a comment.
- **Hashtags = Getting your post noticed.** Hashtags are keywords that allow your post to be searchable. Once you include a hashtag in your post, it will turn blue and

now Instagrammers can click on your hashtag and be taken to other images included in that hashtag. (Finding the right hashtags are key; something we'll go over later.)

- **The best content is aspirational**. People want images that make them feel creative. (Which is great for us, because that's what us Etsians do regularly.) So, skip the overt sales pitch and show pretty pictures of your stuff and you can't go wrong.
- **You can automate the tribe-building.** The secret is to spend most of your time on cool photos and videos. And then use tools — which ones we'll go over later — to help you find followers on auto-pilot. Do this and you'll find a legion of hungry fans for your stuff, without spending hours a day on your marketing.

What's All That Instagram Mumbo-Jumbo Mean?

Don't worry. There's not much lingo. But knowing what these mean will help you understand the lay of the Instagram land:

- **Like**: Symbolized by a heart ♥. You click the heart when you like something. On your posts, you'll see a number next to the heart which shows how many people have "liked" your picture.

- **Home Page**: Where you scroll to view the posts posted by people you follow. (Try saying that sentence three times fast.)

- **Feed**: Your entire photo timeline or gallery. (Similar to Twitter and Facebook.)

- **Tagging**: When you want to notify a fellow Instagrammer with one of your posts. You begin with the "@" and add the username of the person you want to speak to. So if I wanted to reply to a comment by the user @kimkardashian, I would type "@kimkardashian Remind me what the heck it is you do, again…" kim.kardashian will then get a notification or alert you have said something to her. (And her 12 billion followers will focus their ire toward you.)

- **Hashtag**: A word or phrase which has no spaces and is preceded by the "#" symbol. This makes whatever you type after the hashtag searchable and creates a link. Makes it possible to easily find other pictures and users with the same keywords. (Example: #etsy or #HandcraftedSteampunkSoapDish

- **TBT or FBF**: Throwback Thursday, or Flashback Friday, refers to a post on either a Friday or Thursday that is a picture from the past or a previous post. (Great way to recycle previous promos.)

What Else Do I Need to Know?

Well, that's what the rest of this book is for. :)

But, if sugared-up fifteen-year-olds with the

patience of a gnat can figure this platform out, so can you!

Just remember beyond the jargon and photo filters and fancy app features is one simple and timeless principle…

…*"the more you tell, the more you sell."*

And when you're able to share pictures that make people feel good about your products, your aspirations –– even your Jack Russell Terrier who eats headphones — you'll have a good shot at selling a heckuva lot more than you are now.

Which can help you buy more headphones.

Chapter 2: How to Optimize Your Instagram Account for Awesomeness

"I will prepare and someday my chance will come."

-Abraham Lincoln

Before you walk, you gotta crawl. And before you jump into the deep end of the Instagram pool, create an Instagram account maximized for complete Etsy deliciousness.

Some tips outlined below are simple. ("Don't create a profile that sucks and nobody will find.")

Others are a little more ninja and can help you avoid wasted energy on stuff that doesn't move the needle in your business.

But all of them will serve as building blocks for your Etsy sales awesomeness.

So, without further Instagram adieu, let's jump in right with my 5 Steps to Instagram Account Awesomeness:

Step No.1: Download and Register

First things first: you need to get Instagram on your mobile device of choice. Though you can view your Instagram feed on a desktop computer, all the good stuff with Instagram needs to be done on a mobile doohickey contraption thing-y.

Here's what ya do:

1. Download the app. If you're using an Apple device, head over to the App Store. If you're using an Android device, head to the Google Play Store. And if you're using a Windows device, God help you. (Just kidding: use the Windows Phone Store to download the app on your soon-to-be obsolete machine.)

2. Find Instagram. Once the app has downloaded, locate the Instagram app on your device and click the Instagram icon.

3. Register. You can either register with an email address or connect your Instagram account to your Facebook profile. I recommend using email. But I'm weird that way.

4. Enter your email in the space labeled "email." (Duh!) Use the email associated with your Etsy shop. Click "next."

5. Choose a username. You'll want to make this as close to your Etsy account name as possible. This will create a more fluid association between Instagram and Etsy for your buyers. If the username you want isn't available, try adding "the" in front of your user name, or inserting a "." or "_" within your username. If none of these work, you can always add ".com" or ".org" to the end. (Not ideal but can work.)

6. Enter a password. Once you've entered your password, you'll be asked to re-enter the same password again. Click next.

I know, not rocket surgery, as my niece would say. But important.

Step No.2: Make Your Profile Photo All Pretty-Like

Your profile photo is the first thing people see when they check out your profile. It can also turn off people quicker than that awful version of "Summer Nights" you hear at every karaoke session.

That said, getting your profile picture right will enlist a large and loyal Instagram following for ya.

Here's how to take the perfect profile photo:

1. Smile. The first key to a great photo is a big, genuine smile. Data has shown the broader the smile, the more trustworthy and like-able you seem. (Even if you aren't any of those things.) So show us your pearly whites.

2. Use plenty of natural light. When possible, go for an outside picture. One thing to keep in mind with natural light: avoid squinting to look into the camera. If you stand in the shade, make sure it's in full shade, so you don't have shadows on your face.

3. Compose the shot so your face and shoulders fill the frame. People want to see you and your smile, not your outfit or background. Zooming out to see more background can make the photo look busy and not as pleasing to the eye. And on a mobile device it'll look small, small, small.

4. Don't pose. People want to feel like they are looking at someone who is relaxed and natural. They want to see someone they can relate to. Just breathe and be a normal human.

5. Opt for a picture taken by someone else, rather than a selfie. You need not have your photo professionally taken, but you'll look more professional if you have someone else capture the shot. Trust me.

6. Take lots and lots of pictures. It may feel you've gone overboard, but when you take a plethora of pictures, you'll have plenty to choose from, with a better chance at getting that perfect photo. So, keep shooting until you think you've got too many. Then take two more.

7. The ideal size for a profile photo is 180x180 pixels. Keep all the action in the middle.

8. Upload your photo. This is very complicated. It may take you almost twelve seconds to complete. Just click on "edit profile," then "change profile photo" and upload. (See, that wasn't so hard.)

Step No.3: Pack Your Bio With Serious Punch

This is where most of your Instagram damage will be done. Your bio provides a way for followers to get to know you better and form a more emotional connection with your brand. (Nothing connects like stuff about kids and pets. Just sayin'.)

Your profile is the most important space you have to convert casual viewers into long-term buyers.

1. Use your name, if you can. Using your first and last name can help people find you when they are searching for friends to follow. You can either use your name, or you can use the name of your business or Etsy shop. (Ideally, your username should be your Etsy shop name, but see what's available.)

2. Below the bio, you can include a link. Instagram is different from other platforms where you can include links within your profile, not just your posts. With Instagram, this is the only place you may share a link. This is THE place where followers will navigate to your Etsy shop. Enter the URL for your shop here. (Or a landing page, if you have an email marketing funnel set up, which we'll cover in the next chapter.)

3. Use your 4 lines of bio real estate wisely. I don't know how other Instagrammers use this bio spot, but here's what I recommend. First, grab a copy of my Craft Biz Instagram Text Template. (Free copy at CraftBizInsider.com/InstagramBio) Type in the template and copy and paste right into your profile. Remember you want to keep it short and sweet. Avoid the urge to post a myriad of links and text. Use the first line of your bio to introduce your business in a personal, unique way and use the rest of the lines in your bio to give a specific "call to action." ("To get a 25% coupon and be entered to win your very own pair of Steampunk goggles…")

Step No.4: Connect With Friends

More followers beget more followers. And the easiest and best way to have an instant pool of friends is to connect with contacts before you post. Though I can't prove it, Instagram will give you higher visibility if there's a lot of activity around your account right away.

This means you:

1. Connect to people you already know. Find friends and people to follow by using the Facebook and email contacts feature. This can boost your follower count by leaps and bounds.

2. Connect with customers. Let your email list, or fans on other platforms, know you're on Instagram and you'd LOVE to hear from them.

3. Connect Instagram to your other social platforms. On the last page of setting up your profile, before your first post, about half way down, will be slide buttons you can click to turn green and enable Instagram to simultaneously post on the other apps you choose. This is a great way to find more followers and more people who might be interested in your wares. Be careful, though, in case you post something you don't want to get out to your entire tribe.

Step No.5: Drive Juicy Backlinks to Your Instagram Profile

This last one is off-the-beaten path. You'll be tempted to disregard it as a bunch of Internet phooey. But it works and can help your Instagram profile zoom up the Google search results. And it involves purchasing backlinks that point to your Instagram profile page, using craft-specific keywords.

The process works like this:

1. Come up with 2-3 keywords that describe your Etsy store offerings. Such as "steampunk jewelry" or "lavender handmade soap."

2. Head to Fiverr. Purchase 2-3 "SEO" gigs. Doesn't matter what kind, just choose freelancers with high ratings.

3. Give them the keywords and your Instagram profile URL. Then let them build backlinks to your Instagram profile.

Now you won't see results if your Instagram account is just getting started. But you'll see, when somebody searches for your keyword on Google, your Instagram account shows up.

This is like getting FREE Google advertising, without paying for a single click.

Not bad for $15 worth of Internet phooey.

Chapter 2 Action Steps:

- **Download and register for an Instagram account.** Use a mobile device, connect to either your email address or Facebook account, and choose a username (your shop name) that doesn't sound super-spammy.

- **Make your profile all pretty-like**. Don't forget to smile, use plenty of natural light, fill the frame with face and shoulders (no torso shots), take more pics than you think you need, and remember the ideal size for your pic is 500x500 pixels.

- **Pack your bio with serious punch**. This means including your name, a link in your profile (to your Etsy store or email capture page), and four kick-ass lines in your bio that tell followers what you're about — and how to buy your stuff. (Don't forget to use my Craft Biz Instagram Text Template -

CraftBizInsider.com/InstagramBio.)

- **Connect with friends (if you have them)**. Create an instant Instagram following by connecting with people you already know, current customers, and your other social media stalkers.

- **Drive backlinks to your profile**. Increase your Google search engine visibility, for just a couple bucks, by buying "SEO backlink" gigs on Fiverr and sending traffic back to your Instagram profile URL.

Chapter 3: Creating the Ultimate Instagram Profit Funnel

"Success is the sum of small efforts, repeated day in and day out."

-Robert Collier

So now you've got your Instagram account up and running, must mean you're ready to go out there and amass your tribe of Insta-fans, right?

Not quite.

The biggest mistake Etsians make when dipping their toe into the Instagram waters is not having systems in place, before they start, to ensure their efforts are productive and focused on what's important…

…selling crafts!

Because while metrics such as "likes" and "comments" are nice, if we don't have the infrastructure in place — to turn those "likes" and "comments" into leads and customers — then we'll just be spinning our Instagram wheels.

Now, you don't HAVE TO implement the strategies mentioned in this chapter. No one will throw you into Instagram jail if you don't.

And if you've got hours of free time to "engage" on Instagram, and experiment until you find what works, knock yourself out.

But if you'd like to boost the chances your efforts on Instagram lead to more sales — not just "likes" from a Goth 14-year-old with the username @painpoet — then follow this 5-step process to building the ultimate Instagram Etsy marketing funnel:

Step No.1: Steal…Err…Borrow From Others

Before you create a single post on Instagram, it's a good idea to check out other Instagrammers and get a feel for what you want your feed to look like.

This will also give you insight into what you would NEVER want to do, under penalty of law. (Or penalty of a forced viewing of Season 5 of Keeping Up With the Kardashians. Know which one I'd pick.)

This means you should:

1. Check out other Etsians/handcrafters similar to your vibe or specific craft. See what pictures they've posted. What does their profile look like? What's the emotional feel of their content? What are they selling? Not selling? How are they getting users to act? And how could you borrow their techniques?

2. Collect a library of hashtags. Remember those hashtags? Take a stab at searching for words that match your niche or Etsy offering. Collect these hashtags in an excel sheet or text document. This will save you time later on. Trust me.

3. Make a list of influencers. Especially bloggers or anybody who buys a lot of stuff in your craft niche. This could be anybody: journalists, celebs, local shop owners. Anybody who'd have an interest in what you sell. (And who you can "tag" later on when you post.)

Imitation may be the last thing you want to do as an artist, but when you're new to an unfamiliar platform, it's helpful to model your first few posts or initial profile after an Instagrammer whose view you like.

From there you can morph into your own style and change your profile accordingly. After a short time, you'll be able to tell, from experience, what's working for you and your business…and what isn't.

Step No.2: Set Up an Email Capture Landing Page

When starting out, you may want to just send Instagram fans straight to your Etsy shop. And this can work just fine.

But in my experience the most effective, and

profitable, method is to send Instagram traffic to an email landing page — some folks call it a "squeeze page," but I hate that term — in which you offer an incentive, usually a coupon, in exchange for an email address.

So you can market to a subscriber, over and over.

The power of a landing page is its simplicity.

It's a clean, easy-to-read webpage whose primary function is to collect email addresses. Not tout your website or sell your stuff; just get an email address.

And they work well.

Now what you give away is up to you; coupons work for me. But you could do a free sample, or maybe an online video class.

Whatever.

Just know your landing page should include (and only include):

- **A picture** (of the thing you're

giving away)
- **A headline** (letting people know who the freebie is for)
- **A paragraph** (telling people what they need to do to get the freebie)
- **A place** for people to type in their name and email

You can try to create your own landing page if you're technically minded or familiar with all the ins and outs of HTML.

I ain't.

The best and easiest way to create this page is to use a service like LeadPages. I'm an unabashed fan and they make creating simple, beautiful landing pages a cinch.

Though not free, adding leads this way to your funnel can put hundreds, if not thousands, of dollars a month in your pocket.

Step No.3: Get Your Email Stuff Ready

After collecting all those email addresses, what the #%@# do you do with them? This is where an email service, or auto-responder, comes in handy.

An email auto-responder is a tool that lets you store email addresses and send pre-written email sequences to subscribers.

And it can be a real game-changer for your business.

Two of the best out there are MailChimp and Aweber. With MailChimp you can get a free account that allows you to manage up to 2,000 email addresses.

Starting with a free service might be perfect because you might not have gathered a ton of emails to this point. (Though you can only send broadcast emails, or onetime emails, not pre-written stuff.)

If you have a lot of email addresses already, or you want a service that is more user-friendly and robust, go with Aweber. It's what I use, and it works. (And they let you do a 30-day trial for $1, so there's that.)

But the tech ain't the important part, it's the

content. Which I recommend you fill with stuff that tells people who you are, what your story is, and shares your artistic passion.

Leave the overt selling until after you've sent 3-4 emails. (Don't worry, you'll end up selling more in the long run.)

Step No.4: Install "Follow Me" Icons Everywhere

If you have blog or a website connected to your business — and if you don't, why the heck not? — you'll want to add a "follow me on Instagram" icon wherever you can.

Instagram calls these Instagram badges. (No, you don't get to pull people over.)

These badges can help you direct new followers to your Instagram feed and you have different-sized icons to choose from.

To access the badges you can go to your profile and click on your username and then click on "badges." All that's left is to choose your badge, copy the code they provide you with, and paste that code to your website.

Step No.5: Get Thy Analytics and Link Shortener Set Up

I know the terms "analytics" and "link shortener" may conjure images of 10th-grade Math class. (I know it does for me.)

But there's real power in knowing what marketing strategies work, and which don't.

Not just in terms of money, but time and energy.

And if you want to know how many times a link has been clicked on or shared, there's no better method than using Google Analytics and a link-shortener to take the temperature of your business.

And see which of your posts on Instagram are making a difference.

So, I recommend you:

1. Create a Google Analytics account. If you don't already have one.

2. Hire somebody on Fiverr to install Google

Analytics on every page of your website and landing pages. Should cost $5.

3. Poke around Google Analytics for just 10 minutes a day, for the next 30 days. Don't feel like ya gotta master it all at once. Just look at where your traffic is coming from: website, email, Facebook page or Instagram profile. See where your visitors are located or what time of day or day of the week you're getting the most activity. (And which pages are most popular on your site.)

4. Hire somebody on Fiverr to create a Google Analytics Instagram tracking link template for you. If you're tech-y, you can do this yourself; otherwise hire somebody to create the template for you. (It'll look something like: http://www.yourwebsite.com/?utm_campaign=spring&utm_medium=instagram&utm_source=biolink)

5. Using the template, swap out modifiers to change the link being tracked. For example, you could do "Mondaypost_3_11_17" under source or change the medium to "Instagram contest" or "email_1." Whatever. It's your world — we're just living in it!

6. Get a friendly URL. Paste that long, ugly

Google link into a service like Bit.ly and get a friendly URL, such as bit.ly/42365, and then use that link wherever you want. (Instagram posts, profile bio, etc.)

7. Check your Google Analytics to see what's working. And become a small-business expert, without taking a single MBA night course.

Setting up your Instagram account is a huge step in the right direction, but to capitalize on the huge gains Instagram can offer, make that bridge between followers and buyers.

By using some tools above, you'll have taken a giant leap toward selling more stuff, making more money and turning your hobby into an actual, thriving business. (Let's see a Kardashian do that.)

Chapter 3 Action Steps:

- **Get a lay of the land**. Spy on…I mean…study other Etsians on Instagram to see things like how often they post, what they post, what they use for a call-to-action, what hashtags they use, etc. And always be collecting a list of influencers — and super craft fans — you can reach out to at a later date.

- **Set up an email capture page**. This is where the long-term profits are. Use a tool like LeadPages (my favorite tool ever!) to create a simple landing page that gives people a coupon — or some other freebie — in exchange for their email address.

- **Get your email stuff ready**. And by "stuff" we mean sign up for an auto-responder that lets you collect email addresses and send out pre-written (and broadcast) email messages. Aweber and MailChimp are two good, cheap options.

(Game changer!)

- **Install "Follow Me" icons everywhere**. And we mean everywhere! Your website, email signature, other social channels…everywhere!

- **Get thy analytics and link shortener set up**. Though the terms may scare you into thinking you're back in Mr. Flattum's 10th-grade Geometry class, using a combination of Google Analytics, a link shortening service (such as Bit.ly) and somebody on Fiverr to create custom links for you…you can determine what parts of your marketing (including Instagram) are working and which are not.

Chapter 4: 7 Secrets to Awesome (and Profitable) Instagram Content

"Simple is good."

-Jim Henson

This section might be a no-brainer for you. As an artist/Etisan, you (probably) know what good design is. You have an eye for creating beautiful pieces of art that human people want to own. (What my Dad used to call the "pretty, pretty stuff.")

But creating Instagram content that helps you reach your marketing objectives is about more than just making the "pretty, pretty stuff."

It's about telling stories, using the latest Instagram tools to your benefit, and making sure each piece of wonderful, resplendent content doesn't just awe and amaze…

…but inspires (and strongly encourages) followers to act. (Namely, buy your stuff!)

While I can't guarantee I'll be able to show you how to create posts that get shared millions of times in an hour, I can guarantee, if you follow these guidelines, you'll boost your ability to get your crafts (and your Etsy shopping cart) in front of a much-larger audience.

So, here are seven tips for creating awesome, popular, and (hopefully) profitable Instagram content:

Secret No.1: Begin with the End in Mind

The best map in the world won't help you if you don't know where you're going. And in this extended Instagram metaphor, it's important to have an idea for what you hope to accomplish with your posts.

- Is the goal of your post to get more

followers?

- Have users share your post on their feed? (And engage with your account?)

- Is it to establish the aura of your brand and what you create?

- Is it to get people to sign up for your email list?

- Or to increase sales?

Different posts can have different goals and should.

I find most of my sales happen at night and on weekends. So, that's when I focus my overt "pitch" posts. ("New steampunk lamp — 10% off!")

But the rest of the time, the afternoons, is when I'll do more evergreen, inspirational stuff. (Quotes, behind-the-scenes, etc.)

But you need to do what works for you.

I like to have an overall mix of 75% feel-good

content — stuff that doesn't "sell" — and 25% "Hey, go buy something…"

But you may find a different mix works for you.

You want to use Google Analytics — remember that from last chapter? — to help you find what works best for your customers.

Just remember: "The confused mind says 'no.'" Don't give followers too many things to do in each post or they won't do anything at all.

Secret No.2: Follow the Rules of Design

Most of these tips will be quick, unnecessary reminders of what you already know. (You're an artist.) But some of you may need brushing up on your graphic-design skills.

If so, here are a couple of guidelines to…well…guide you:

- **Rule of thirds -** Divide your shot (or video) using six imaginary lines; three horizontal, three vertical. Insure your subject falls into the top intersections for the most pleasing shot.

- **White space -** Use white space — or empty space — in your shot to draw attention to your subject.

- **Resolution** - Make sure your photo is crisp and clear. Sometimes this can be fixed in editing, sometimes not. Best to do when composing your shot.

- **Contrast -** The more contrast you have in your picture, the more likely it'll grab attention. (If you're doing video, make sure you're shooting with the sun and/or light behind the camera.)

- **The Right Saturation -** You want to go for photos with high saturation. Unless you're adding text, then a more muted picture can make for a better background.

Secret No.3: Don't Stress About the Camera

If you already own an expensive DLR camera,

and you're good at taking pics with it, use it. Don't spend $2500 on a new camera, unless you want to.

The camera you have on your smartphone is more than adequate, and way more convenient, than a big, large HD camera.

But that's just my opinion.

Secret No.4: Let Free Apps Help

There are solid, free design apps that can make your posts pop. Besides design apps, Instagram has a few apps in its collection to help you create collage posts or different kinds of videos.

Let's look at them in a little more detail:

- **Canva** - A free app that allows you to add text over photos, find and use millions of stock photos, add icons and edit photos with filters.

- **Pablo by Buffer** - Very similar to Canva. Pablo is more about helping you create a social media post while Canva can design a myriad of images. Still a helpful add to your arsenal.

- **Hyperlapse** - Allows you to create polished, time-lapsed videos. An awesome tool if you want to publish a video showcasing your process.

- **Layout** - Another Instagram app where you create collages of photos from your library or create spur-of-the-moment collages.

- **Boomerang** - Creates a video, few seconds in length, that repeats on a loop. The result is a fun, mesmerizing product that your followers will love. (Especially those Millennials with no attention span.)

Secret No.5: When in Doubt, Tell Stories & Stir Emotions

Okay, so we've covered all the tools, apps and design stuff that will help you create great content. But what should the content look like? What kinds of posts should you create that will build a massive audience?

No matter whether the end goal of a particular post is to get more people into your art or having people buy your stuff, the most successful Instagram content is that which gets people to feel something — strongly — and helps them understand your artistic journey better.

Stories and emotions. That's what it's all about. Stories and emotions.

Now, I'm no expert, but here are a couple of ideas when creating buzz-worthy Instagram content:

- **Let followers into the studio**. Show them a shot of your materials or where you do your crafting. This allows people a behind-the-scenes look where the magic happens. And people buy magic.
- **Time-lapse video.** Take a sped-up video of you painting your picture, throwing a pot or crafting your jewelry, and share it with your tribe.
- **Answer a question.** Offer a tip. Show off a trick with your craft. Give insight into your process and inspire followers to perfect their own creations.

- **Place a quote on top of a picture.** These work well. I do not understand why, but they do. Use something that speaks to your brand and isn't too clichéd or corny.

- **Share something personal.** Occasionally share something about your life that has nothing to do with your creations. Share a picture of your kids or your latest skydiving expedition. Or that Jack Russell Terrier that ate a throw pillow. Don't go too personal, just keep it fun and visual.

- **User-generated posts.** One of the easiest posts to do is one you don't do at all. Encourage people who purchased your art to post about it. You can do this by asking for it in one of your posts and encouraging followers to use a specific hashtag. If you think your followers need additional encouragement to share, you can offer a discount or a free item for the winning post.

These are just suggestions; you may (probably do) have more creative ideas for your content. Just ask yourself does this post a) tell a story and b) stir emotions? If so, you're on the right Instagram track.

Secret No.6: When in Doubt, Just "RePost" Somebody Else's Stuff

One of the easiest methods for creating Instagram content is to NOT create it all. But "repost" Instagram content that somebody else posts.

You don't want to rely only on content that OTHER people create. (Wc want people to…you know…check out our stuff.) But there's nothing wrong with filling your feed with other awesome stuff that people (not named you) create.

The old way to do this used to be to take a screenshot of a post on Instagram, with your phone, and then repost it. (Ugh, who wants to work that hard.)

These days there's a far better option, and it's with a simple (and free) tool called Repost.

With the "Repost" app, you fire it up, look for Instagram content you think is interesting (and your would-be customers would gravitate towards) and then "repost" it.

Now, at the time of this writing, you can't schedule "reposting" just yet. (What I do is find interesting posts and then "favorite" them, so I can repost later.)

Secret No.7: Develop a Consistent Look & Feel

So, this is more of an advanced tip, but don't worry you're gonna be an advanced Instagram marketer in no time, so I want to share it with you!

And that is: a big mistake I see with Etsians is a lack of focus. (Not just on Instagram, but across the whole marketing board.)

You want to hone in on a specific look and feel that matches your vibe, your Etsy brand, your personality.

Some homework earlier, on other profiles, should help. You can do this by choosing one or two "emotion adjectives" that encompass what your business is about.

For our store, the adjectives we go for are "steampunk couture" and "modern vintage." (I know those may not make sense to YOU, and they sound paradoxical, but they make sense for us. And that's what's important.)

Every branding/marketing decision is then filtered through your emotion adjectives. Does this font, color, style, email, piece of sales copy fit in with "steampunk couture?" If not, we skip it.

Here are items to consider when creating the visual look of your brand:

- **Choose a font that flows with the feel of your brand and stick with it.** Bonus points if you use the same font on your website, blog, shop and other marketing materials.

- **Select a color palette** and use those colors as a primary theme in your photos, blog and listings. As a steampunk artisan, for me, it's all about earth tones and metallics. But for you, it might be pastels. (Though if it is, I beg you to reconsider.)

- **Use the same Instagram filters again and again.** Stick to just two or three, at most. (In the next chapter I'll go over my favorite

Instagram filters to use.)

- **Come up with your own terms and jargon.** People love to belong to tribes. So give them tribe-specific phrases and jargon that only insiders will understand. (They'll love you for it.)

Again, I'm no branding expert. But research suggests the more a company can make every aspect of their visual marketing consistent and connected, the better they do. And we're a company, dammit! (Even if that company only has one employee.)

Chapter 4 Action Steps:

- **Begin with the end in mind**. Come up with one goal for each post. The author recommends having a mix of 75% content posts and 25% promotional posts. (But the author also thought Cyndi Lauper was gonna be a bigger star than Madonna, so what does he know?)

- **Follow the rules of design**. When shooting photos and videos for Instagram remember the rule of thirds, use plenty of white space, use saturation (with filters), and crank up the contrast to make your content eye-catching.

- **Don't stress the camera**. Your phone will work just fine. Trust me.

- **Let the free apps help**. Some of my faves include: Canva, Pablo, Hyperlapse, Layout and Boomerang. (But new ones are created every minute.)

- **Tell stories, stir emotions**. Some great ways to do this include: behind-the-scenes content, time-lapse videos of your artistry, quotes on pictures, personal stuff, and user-generated content.

- **If you have no stories, repost somebody else's story.** Use the "repost" app to share cool content with your followers. And fill your feed with goodness, creating nothing yourself.

- **Develop a consistent look and feel**. Come up with 1-2 emotion adjectives that describe your brand and make sure your font, colors, filters and jargon all fit.

Chapter 5: The How, What, Where and When of Instagram Posting Amazing-ness

"Action may not always bring happiness, but there is no happiness without action."

-Benjamin Disraeli

We've talked the big-picture strategy of Instagram marketing. (Creating a funnel, devising content, making sure your branding doesn't look like you're in the midst of a psychotic break, etc.)

But now we're gonna dive into the nuts-and-bolts. The step-by-step blueprint for HOW to post photos and videos on Instagram. (And ensure they find the BIGGEST audience possible.)

Before we get started, I have to reiterate I am NOT an Instagram expert. This is what worked for me. You may find ANOTHER process works better for you.

But I encourage you to give this a try, to try *something.* (Then do your recon to see what works best for your particular slice of the Etsy world.)

With that heavy-handed caveat out of the way, let's jump right into the trenches with this 5-step blueprint to Instagram post awesomeness:

Step No.1: Deciding When to Post

The best times to post on Instagram, I've found, are:

- 5:00 p.m. (EST)
- 10:00 p.m. (EST)
- 1:00-2:00 a.m. (EST)

I've tested this a bunch, and this seems to work best. Which makes sense; afternoons and evenings are when people want to shut off their brains and look at pretty pictures.

But this assumes your audience is in the general United States. If you sell only to the Pacific Northwest, or the island of Borneo, tweak these times. Still, as guidelines go, the 5pm - 10pm - 1am is a good benchmark.

But wait…does this mean you have to stay up until 1:00 a.m.?

No.

Though you're not able to, at the time I write these words, to schedule posts through the Instagram app, you can use a social media management tool, such as HootSuite, to schedule your posts into the future.

HootSuite is my particular scheduling weapon of choice — I use it for my Twitter, Facebook and Instagram scheduling — and it's FREE. (Which is awesome.) HootSuite has a detailed look at how to do this on their blog. You can check it out at CraftBizInsider.com/ScheduleInstagram.

Now, as for the best days of the week to post, you can't go wrong focusing most of your energies on (in descending order of effectiveness):

- Wednesdays
- Thursdays
- Tuesdays

This isn't a hard-fast rule. I sell MORE crafts on the weekends. People feel less frantic then; more in the mood to buy stuff.

But I get more Instagram ACTIVITY — likes, shares and follows — on Wednesdays, Thursdays and Tuesdays.

Don't know why, just the way it is.

Again, test things to see what works best for you. (But just try *something.*)

Step No.2: Deciding How Often to Post

This is the number one question I get from Etsians about posting on Instagram. How often should I post?

And I get it; it was my number one question,

too.

Just know it's up to you what you feel you can, and can't, handle. No ONE single post is gonna make-or-break your business. Every bit helps.

My particular posting schedule looks something like:

- 3x a day - Tuesday-Thursday (5pm; 10pm; 1am)
- 1x a day - Friday - Monday (5pm)

And following my general 75% content, 25% promo ratio, this means my total output looks something like…

- 13 total posts a week
- 9 content-driven posts a week (quotes, inspirational, pretty stuff, reposts etc.)
- 4 promotional posts a week (asking followers to act that helps me make money or boost follower counts)

You don't have to do that much, at first. And let nobody tell you you have to post 5x a day. (It's a waste of time.)

What you want is a mix that serves you and your business, not send you to the loony bin.

Step No.3: Find Your Raw Material

Once you've got a good idea of when you'll post — and how often you'll post — then it's time to upload that photo or video of yours and experiment with some tools Instagram puts at your disposal.

When creating a new Instagram post, you have three content choices:

- **Library** - Photos and videos you've already created
- **Photo** - In which you take a photo on-the-spot and turn it into a post
- **Video**- In which you shoot a video on-the-spot and turn it into a post

I prefer to shoot photos and videos beforehand, stuff related to my products. But use whatever process works best for you. (And whatever helps you get more Instagram awesomeness out there.)

Step No.4: Choose Your Filter

Instagram filters are kinda like the tax code;

they're important and anybody understands them.

But if you can navigate through the noise — and find filters you like — you can add serious juice to your Instagram posts. (Note: Be careful using filters on video posts, at least until you get a sense of how they work. They can look god-awful.)

As we discussed earlier, it's a good idea to pick a few go-to filters and use them in your posts on Instagram. This will establish a consistent feel and look of your brand.

But which filters should you use? This is a subjective question — and one that causes more Instagram debates than you'd think — but here are a few tried-and-true options I recommend:

- **Early Bird** - The most forgiving filter. It makes the subject look more "bronzed" and "golden" than usual. It's the most popular filter out there for a reason. Early Bird makes every shot look dramatic and interesting. (Even if it isn't either.)
- **X-Pro II** - The go-to filter if you want your picture to look dramatic and have dark edges around the corner. This will give your shot the look of an old-fashioned photograph.
- **Valencia** - Perfect filter if your photo is

darker than you like or you need more of a washed-out background for the text to stand out. This filter will take a "dark" photo and boost the "lightness" of your pics, which can be perfect for product launches, event promotions, and links to content. A dramatic filter, without the "undead" look.

- **Hefe** - If your picture has lots of color, and you need sharpness and vibrancy, this filter is perfect.
- **Brannan** - If you're going for that artistic, discolored (post-apocalyptic wasteland) look, where the color is washed out, then this is your filter.
- **Nashville** - Ideal if you want to use a subtle filter.

Step No.5: Create Those Captions

Let's talk captions. I know the photos (and videos) are the eye candy that catches the attention of users, but it's captions where the real "selling" happens.

That said, "less" is more for captions. Couple things to keep in mind:

- **Instagram allows a max of 2,200 characters.** If you need more than that, you're doing something wrong.

- **Your caption will be truncated, with ellipses, after three lines.** So make sure you get the most important information early on.
- **Captions are great for asking people to do stuff.** Ask questions or use language that encourages followers to comment or share.
- **Keep captions short and sweet.** Your post gets 66% more traffic when your post is fewer than eighty characters. Your post gets 86% more traffic when your post is fewer than forty characters. Keep. It. Short.
- **Use quotes over pictures for boosted impact.** (Use a free tool like Canva to handle this.) Just keep them fresh and cliché free.
- **Try to use 4-5 hashtags per post.** That seems to be the sweet spot; far better than one or zero. Use research to find out which hashtags to use, but #Etsy should be one. You can put 30 hashtags in your post, but I don't recommend it. (Too spammy.)

Step No.6: Remember What Makes You Unique

You've been asked, throughout this book, to look at successful Instagrammers within your field and model what's worked for them.

While this is still an essential and critical piece to

creating your own popular Instagram campaign, it's vital you bring your own flavor to whatever you do. (Even if this hapless author tells you to do the opposite.)

This means looking at your art, at your life, and asking:

- What makes you unique?
- What do you offer no one else does?
- What do you love about where you live or how you live your life day?

Bring these details to the forefront of your posts. The quirkier and more unique and oddball your posts are, the more people will relate to it. (No matter how many times a day you post.)

Chapter 5 Action Steps:

- **Decide WHEN to post -** The biggest-impact posting times on Instagram are 5:00 p.m./1o:00 p.m./1:00 a.m. — with Wednesdays, Thursdays and Tuesdays the best days of the week to focus on. Don't worry about staying up until 1 a.m.; just use a free scheduler, like Hootsuite, to set 'em up beforehand.

- **Decide HOW OFTEN to post -** My schedule runs 3x a day (Tuesday-Thursday) and 1x a day (Friday-Monday). But do what works best for you. And don't stress out if you're not doing it as much, at first.

- **Find your RAW material -** Ya got three choices: library (photos and vids you already created), photos you create in the app and videos you create in the app. I prefer to create stuff outside the Instagram app, but I'm weird that way.

- **Choose your FILTER -** Some of the best filters to use are Early Bird (most forgiving), X-Pro II (dark edges), Valencia (lightens your shot), Hefe (sharp colors), and Brannan (artsy). But find what works for you and stick with it.

- **Create your CAPTIONS** - Where the real marketing magic is. Keep 'em short (under 40 characters, fs possible), use quotes, and aim for 4-5 hashtags per post.

- **Be UNIQUE** - Think about ways to express your unique and quirky personality. Take risks and you'll be rewarded.

Chapter 6:
4 Keys to Building a Rabid Army of Instagram Followers

"It's hard to lead a Calvary charge if you think you look funny on a horse."

-Adlai Stevenson

What's an Instagram account with nobody to see it?

Having an engaging profile, beautiful posts and a cohesive brand are critical. But without that all-important follower, none of those pretty filters or engaging posts will matter if you don't have folks consuming your content. (And buying your stuff.)

There's no magic button to getting followers — although later in the chapter I will show you something damn close — but if you stick with systems that work, before you know it, you'll have a bigger Instagram following than you ever thought possible. (Who knows; maybe they'll do a reality show about you next!)

So, here are four strategies to building a rabid, obsessed and passionate Instagram tribe all your own:

Tribe Source No.1: Friends and Family

We talked about this earlier, but one of the fastest, and easiest ways to build your Instagram following is through your email and Facebook contacts.

You can do this either when you create your Instagram account — you'll be asked, during set-up, if you'd like to add friends from Facebook or email — or later on after you've done some posting. But either way you should add as many people as you can with this strategy.

Another super-simple strategy for boosting follower counts is to use the “Discover People” option. This lets you find people you may have missed in setting up your account and gives suggestions of other Instagrammers — who are connected with people who you follow or who follow you — that you want to reach out to.

Don’t worry if you miss somebody; Instagram will keep pestering…err…reminding you of folks you may know on Instagram. Just make sure you do this initial step, at some point, to ensure your account looks lively and vibrant from the get-go.

Tribe Source No.2: Fans and Customers

It’s important to link your Instagram profile to the other ways your customers engage with you, such as your website, email newsletters, and other social media properties.

On your website, make sure you have at least one “Follow me on Instagram” button on every page of your site. (Done by one of those tech-y types on Fiverr.)

I've found the best real estate for these types of Instagram-sharing icons are the website sidebar, footer of all blog posts and "About Me" pages on your website.

But you can also add that same button to Tumblr posts, Twitter bios, email signatures, newsletters, business cards, message board profiles, Facebook page links…anywhere you can think of.

One quick tip: Incentivize people to follow you on Instagram by running a contest where you pick a new follower each month to get something cool.

Do that and your follower count will grow in no time.

Tribe Source No.3: Shout outs

To build a loyal and massive following, you have to interact with others on Instagram. (Sorry, being a hermit doesn't boost follower count.)

This means choosing the Instagrammers you identified earlier, and referred to for inspiration, and then interact with them on a semi-regular basis.

Here's how I recommend you do it:

- Each day choose three Instagram followers you found in your research. (Profiles whose followers you think would make good customers.)

- On one of the accounts, "like" a post — then repost to your account.

- On one of the other accounts, make a thoughtful comment — then repost to your account.

- On one of the other accounts, usually the one with the highest engagement, compliment them and invite them to check out your stuff. (Example: "Hey @ladygaga — Love your stuff. If you haven't already, checkout my Steampunk Jewelry page. Love to know what ya think!")

This should take only 2-3 minutes, but if done consistently you'll be shocked how quickly it can make a difference.

The BEST TIME to do this three-pronged attack is during the hours of 5:00PM-10:00PM EST.

It's quick and something you can do during that episode of *Law and Order: Special Task Force Unit Squadron.*

But this slow-burn method of Instagram engagement can be a great way to show appreciation, while getting you high engagement rates and an elevated follower count.

Tribe Source No.4: Follower Automation

This last tribe-building source may offend your delicate sensibilities. And if it does, I apologize, and you can fast-forward to the next chapter for more kind-hearted strategies and suggestions that don't require you to go against your digital marketing morals.

But I've found the quickest method for gaining Instagram fans is also the easiest. (And it's a method that doesn't require you make a single post.) It's by using an automated interaction tool called Follow Liker.

In the Instagram universe, every time a user's account gets a like, follow, tag or comment, they get a notification. And when they check out that notification, and see a profile, like yours, that appears relevant and interesting, they'll follow you. The key is interaction — consistent, slow interaction — that you automate so you build your tribe .

Sounds great. How does it work? Basically, you install Follow Liker on your computer, decide how many people you'll follow each day, decide how many people you'll unfollow (and after how long), and then let the computer run in the background…and you're done!

Now, the setup is self-explanatory, but if you end up using Follow Liker, here are a couple guidelines to keep in mind:

- **Don't use the tool every day.** Take one day off a week. (I take Mondays off.)
- **Don't use the tool overnight.** When you sleep, so should the tool.
- **When getting started, follow only 100-150**

people per day and like only 200 photos a day. After a month, you can ramp this up to following 500 people a day and liking 400 photos a day. But increase slowly.

- **When getting started, set a delay of 60-65 seconds** between actions. Then reduce to about 30 seconds. Build slowly.

- **Don't use FollowLiker to comment.** Just like and follow. Bit too risky asking it to comment.

- **Don't unfollow over 100 people per day.** Otherwise you'll risk the ire of the Instagram police.

FollowLiker is not a free tool. (And it may not be in line with your marketing sensibilities.) But I've found nothing works quite so well — and quickly — to boost my follower count than this tool, just under $100. (You can even use it on Twitter or Pinterest, which can come in handy.)

But even if you don't have an interest in plunking down money for Follow Liker, the principle is still the same. Constant interaction — and appreciation for other Instagrammers — will get you noticed.

And if you're able to devote just 10-15 minutes a day to Instagram interaction, you'll find your follower count — and most likely your Etsy sales — rise.

Chapter 6 Action Steps:

- **Reach out to friends and family** - Look for new Instagram followers by using your email and Facebook contacts. (This can boost your follower count by hundreds.)

- **Reach out to current fans and customers** - Place "follow me on Instagram" icons on your website and other social media channels. (Bonus points if you run a contest where new followers get entered to win something cool.)

- **Interact and give shout outs** - Look over your Instagram research — or use hashtags — each day to find a post you can "like," a post you can comment on, and a user profile you can give a shout out to. (With a suggestion they check out your profile.)

- **Automate your following -** Though it may not sound ethical — don't worry, it is; you should see what other crazy stuff is on Instagram — one of the best tools for boosting your follower count is an automation tool such as FollowLiker. (Just keep your follow/unfollow limits low and conservative.)

Chapter 7: Contests, QR Codes and VAs…Oh My!

"Change is hardest in the beginning, messiest in the middle, and best at the end."

-Robin Sharma

Look at you, Instagram expert!

Come on now, don't be bashful. At this point you have a more solid and expansive knowledge of Instagram than most anybody in the world. (And more than any other Etsy shop owner.)

And you have everything in your Instagram arsenal to promote your brand, grow your following and boost your bottom-line with ninja marketing strategies.

But…

…there will come a time when your Instagram education will plateau. When you'll get results and you'll wonder: what more can you do? (I know you may not believe me, but it will happen.)

And when you're ready to take that next step, I encourage you give these strategies a try. (Or at least a thorough look-see.)

Not all of them will be game-changers — and they are best left until you've got your Instagram footing under you — but these advanced strategies can be, when used effectively with Instagram, a great way to move the needle in your business…big-time!

So, here are three pillars to completing your Ph.D. in Instagram Marketing Studies and help you boost the success of your Etsy business:

Pillar No.1: Instagram Contests

I love contests. I love 'em so much they should be pillars one, two, and three.

That's because contests are the perfect way to build emotional investment in your brand, expand your reach, boost your email subscriber list and (eventually) sell a heckuva lot more stuff.

The reason is simple: people hate being sold to, but they love to play games. Sometimes it doesn't even matter what yer giving away; people just want to win stuff.

This is a technique you will want to wait to use until you have at least a thousand followers. Otherwise the return on your investment won't be as awesome as it could be. (Follow the strategies outlined in the last chapter and getting a thousand followers shouldn't be a problem.)

Once you have a solid base of followers, try to aim for running a contest once every three months. More than that and you can fatigue your followers.

But stick with that once every three months and

you'll love the huge boost in sales and leads you (more-than-likely) will get.

So, how do you run an Instagram contest? Here's the four-step process I follow each time:

1. Choose an enticing prize. Maybe you created a new style of mug and want to showcase it to the masses. Or you've planned a new glaze you're proud of. Offer it up as the prize. Gift cards can also work great. (Especially if it's a gift card to your online store.) But whatever it is: make it good.

2. Announce the rules of the contest in an Instagram post. Generally, it'll be action that requires followers to a) Upload a photo of them expressing themselves or using your product and b) Using a designated contest hashtag. (Such as #steampunketsycontest)

3. Track the hashtag. It's important you choose a unique hashtag. #SummerFun might sound like a great way to describe your contest, but it'll be a nightmare figuring out who entered your contest.

4. Select a winner. There are a lot of free websites that will randomly select a winner for you. I like RandomResult.com.

5. Announce the winner. You can do this either through a specific Instagram post and/or direct message to the winner yourself. (Best of all, announcing the winner gets people excited for the next contest.)

Okay, Charles, sounds good. But what types of contests can I run?

I'm so glad you asked…

Types of Contests

Here are some of the different variations I've tried and had success with:

- Have people comment, like or share to enter a contest
- Have people VOTE on an item of yours (with the winning item going on sale at deep discount)
- Have people tag their friends (Example: "Tag a friend who is into pottery…") — This contest is so popular it's got a

dedicated hashtag — #TagAFriend

- Any fun and visually interesting (though legal) activity you can dream up to have your followers do

You make great art and people deserve to find that art. And with a contest you can push through that usual marketing resistance people have…and cut to that most powerful and primal motivator…

…The desire to win free loot!

Pillar No.2: QR Codes

This marketing tool isn't exclusively for Instagram. But I bring it up because it's a powerful tool that can be used with your Instagram account — or with any aspect of your marketing funnel — to devastating effect.

So, a QR code is a piece of black-and-white mumbo-jumbo code that looks like a blurry chessboard but works like a barcode.

You've seen one at your local restaurant.

And the way they work is this:

- You create the QR code

- You place the QR code somewhere (either in physical or digital form)

- Somebody scans the QR code with their phone

- An action is taken (The user is signed up for an email list, enters a contest, etc.)

What makes this strategy so powerful is how easy it is. The person scans the QR code — whether on a flyer at your craft booth or on the back of your business card — and the person has been entered into your funnel. (At whatever point you choose.)

Now there are many ways to use QR codes with your marketing, but some of my faves include sending code scanners to my:

- Instagram profile
- Facebook page
- Twitter feed (or maybe a Favorited Twitter list of some of my great reviews)

- Amazon store page
- Social media contest page (including Instagram!)
- Etsy store (duh!)
- Facebook fan
- Popular post on my blog
- Sign-up page for my e-newsletter
- A coupon code giveaway page
- Anywhere you think of

I know what you're thinking; but isn't creating a QR code hard?

Not! All ya gotta do is:

1. Find a QR code generator. There are a lot of QR code websites and apps out there. Some free; some have in-app purchases or cost a small amount to buy upfront. If you're going the website direction, I recommend Kaywa - http://qrcode.kaywa.com/. If you'd rather use an app, I'd suggest "QR Scanner."

2. Enter your URL. Once you install the app or visit the QR website, enter into a text box the URL you want attached to the QR code and then hit the create button. (Don't forget to add a tracking link, so you can make sure your QR code campaign is working.) In a few seconds, you'll have your own QR code!

3. Install the QR code anywhere you want! I love to use 'em in places like business cards, craft fair flyers, mailings to customers, newsletters, brick-and-mortar shops, and anywhere you can think of.

The first time you do this, and you realize how easy it is, just sit back and say to yourself: "My old pal, Charles, was right."

Which he was. :)

Pillar No.3: Instagram Stories (or the Future)

I almost didn't include this pillar. Not because it's not important, but because I'm so NEW to using it myself, and didn't want to steer you wrong.

But I want to just plant a seed in your brain. And that is…

- People love video (especially live video)
- Facebook loves what people love
- Facebook owns Instagram

- Facebook is gonna do a lot more with video on Instagram

Now I know Facebook has its own live video service, known as "Facebook Live." Which is great. But I think far less people know about Instagram stories — the Instagram version of live video — which represents a real opportunity for us Etsians.

Why should you use Instagram Stories? Well, according to Kristi Hines, of Social Media Examiner, the tool "allows you to create media that appears at the top of your followers' news feeds for 24 hours."

Let me say that again.

You create a tiny piece of content and it stays in your follower's feed for 24 hours. (Better than any Instagram ad you could ever create.)

The downside is, this video will disappear from your main feed after 24 hours. But this makes it ideal for things like:

- Demoing a new product
- Showing a behind-the-scenes look at your

operation

- Doing a live Q&A
- Celebrating a milestone in your business
- Promoting a contest

The tricky part is figuring out how to do it. (At least for me it was tricky.) Here's what you do:

- Click on the Your Story profile photo (look for the + (plus) sign) at the top of your Instagram news feed.
- Choose one of three options — live (video disappears after broadcast), normal (disappears after 24 hours), and boomerang (creates a time-lapse video from your photos.)
- Click on "start video"
- Record video to your heart's content
- Click "end" to…well…end the video

I prefer the "normal" mode — the one that sticks around for 24 hours. But if you have a lot of followers and want to do more live chats and Q&As, then "live video" might be a better way to go.

Again: I'm no expert. I offer these tips as a future-looking crackpot.

I encourage you to get started now, to experiment with live video on Instagram in these early days, so you and your craft business can take advantage of the fact hardly anybody (and that includes the big dumb corporations) is using this feature to its fullest potential yet.

Chapter 7 Action Steps:

- **Familiarize yourself with what you can — and can't — do with an Instagram contest**. Be sure to choose a great prize, announce the rules upfront, pick a unique hashtag, select a winner, and announce the winner. Good contest ideas include having people comment, like, vote or tag their friends to enter.

- **Explore how QR codes can help your marketing**. They're easy to use; just paste a link into a QR code generator, create the code, place the code, and let the magic happen. Great uses include placing QR codes on business cards, flyers, booths, social media profiles, store pages, blog posts…and coupon code giveaways.

- **Dip your toe into the Instagram stories pool**. Though I'm no expert (yet), I have a feeling Instagram stories (Instagram's version of live video) is gonna take off big-time. I prefer the "normal" version which helps keep your live video in user's feed for 24 hours. Great for product launches and live Q&As.

A Final Word

"The only worthwhile journey is the one within."

-Rainier Maria Rilke

Doing new things, especially new things in front of strangers, can be scary. That's especially true when putting one's clumsy, tentative, uncertain foot forward and promoting your wares on a platform as strange — and seemingly shallow — as Instagram.

I've tried throughout this book to demystify some of the quirks of the Instagram eco-system, and attempted to give you strategies and shortcuts to reduce your learning curve.

To help you stay on the Instagram marketing path. And not get up-ended in the brambles.

But if you try this Instagram stuff out, you will make mistakes. You will do things that don't work. That nobody responds to. That are a complete waste of time.

I encourage you to stick with it. Look at what other people are doing on Instagram. See how you can package your creative vision in a way that tantalizes Instagrammers…and compels them to learn more about you and your products.

If you do, the most marvelous thing will happen. You'll start to enjoy Instagram. You'll love the colors, the spectacle, the speed with which people react and respond to your posts.

And as world gets more visual, fast, and attention-challenged, you'll find Instagram the perfect intersection between art and technology. And gives you a foundation of followers (and future customers) who will not only give you recognition and appreciation for your artistry…

…But hopefully you give a full-time living doing what you love. (Isn't that worth combing through a couple of inane selfies?)

Thank you so much for taking this journey with me and I wish you luck in your future Instagram marketing endeavors.

If you'd like to drop me a line, just ping me over at charles@craftbizinsider.com.

A Special FREE Gift for You!

If you'd like FREE instant access to my special report "Top 10 Marketing Tools Every Etsy Seller Should Use" then head over to **CraftBizInsider.com/Free**.

(What else you gonna do? Watch another "Twilight" movie?!)

DISCLAIMER AND/OR LEGAL NOTICES: Every effort has been made to accurately represent this book and it's potential. Results vary with every individual, and your results may or may not be different from those depicted. No promises, guarantees or warranties, whether stated or implied, have been made that you will produce any specific result from this book. Your efforts are individual and unique, and may vary from those shown. Your success depends on your efforts, background and motivation.

The material in this publication is provided for educational and informational purposes only and is not intended as medical advice. The information contained in this book should not be used to diagnose or treat any illness, metabolic disorder, disease or health problem. Always consult your physician or health care provider before beginning any nutrition or exercise program. Use of the programs, advice, and information contained in this book is at the sole choice and risk of the reader.

Printed in Great Britain
by Amazon